GW00418005

Heritage of Aotearoa

THE BUSH PRESS HISTORIC PLACES OF NEW ZEALAND

THE BUSH PRESS HISTORIC PLACES OF NEW ZEALAND

Heritage of Aotearoa

TEXT AND ILUSTRATIONS BY

GORDON ELL

The Bush Press of New Zealand

DEDICATION

Remembering those who have gone before:
recognising their presence in the present;
helping to preserve our past for posterity.

First published in 1998 by
THE BUSH PRESS OF NEW ZEALAND

Designed by Gordon Ell, and produced by The Bush Press in Auckland, New Zealand

Printed in Hong Kong through
Bookprint Consultants Ltd, Wellington, N.Z.

Published by Bush Press Communications Ltd,
P.O.Box 33-029, Takapuna, Auckland 9, N.Z.

ISBN 0-908608-78-0 (Hardbound Edition)
ISBN 0-908608-83-7 (Limpback Edition)

COVER PICTURES: Front cover, typical Northland countryside with pa on the hill. Back cover, rock drawing, Timpendean, North Canterbury.

FRONTISPIECE: Wall of river stones retains the terraces of a fortified Maori settlement now buried by forest regrowth; Koru Pa, Taranaki.

TITLE PAGE: Unusual stone store carved in pumice at the Buried Village, Wairoa, Lake Tarawera.

Contents

Acknowledgements

THE PHOTOGRAPHS AND NOTES in this book have been gathered over 15 years or more, wherever and whenever the opportunity arose to record some interesting aspect of the landscape of pre-European New Zealand. Consequently I have become indebted to many people, landowners, archaeologists, and Maori, who have given access to places and information. Some of the earlier material was gathered while making documentaries for television: for access I must thank again the owners of Great Mercury Island and the Tahanga basalt quarry; also the private owners of the pa sites at Whitianga, Pouerua, and those on the Papamoa Hills. Elsewhere, a number of landowners have provided public access across their land, to sites of importance, such as the Timpendean shelter in North Canterbury. Most of the sites in this book, however, are viewable from public roads or are managed in the public interest, notably those in Auckland city and Taranaki.

Among the scientific community I must particularly thank David Simmons, sometime ethnologist and assistant director at Auckland War Memorial Museum, whose researches led me to make the original television films. He has long been unstinting in his sharing of knowledge of sites and events. A number of archaeological teams and individuals connected with the Anthropology Department at the University of Auckland further facilitated the earlier pictures. Several individuals have helped in the field including, over the years, Brian Hurst, Carol Long, and Karen McMillan our helpful guide on the Chatham Islands. Advice on specific pictures and places was tendered, among others, by Dr Nigel Prickett and John Klaricich of Waiwhatawhata.

Finally I should thank my family, Ruth, Fiona and Sarah, who suffered frequent stops on holiday travels to capture many of these pictures. Ruth, in particular, shared a number of journeys and subsequently read proofs, sorted pictures, and helped with production. Thank you all.

GORDON ELL, Takapuna 1998.

MAORI PA SITE

The ruins of a Maori fortress atop a hill creates one of the quintessential landscapes of northern New Zealand. This pa, near Lake Omapere inland from the Bay of Islands, can be traced by the banks and ditches which interrupt the natural curves of the hill. The pa is one of more than 5000 still detectable in the North Island landscape.

Author's Note

THE SUBJECTS OF THIS BOOK speak largely for themselves. My job has been to gather a representative selection of landscape features which reflect the past of Aotearoa. Their meaning, beyond the physically obvious, lies with those who created them.

The purpose of this volume, and those which are to come on the historic landscapes of New Zealand, is to capture the fast-fading physical signs of the people who have gone before. That past, in many ways, has shaped our present and may in valuable ways, help shape our future. While some of these images may have special and particular meaning for local Maori, they also bring a broader character to the landscape we all share. By identifying such features as Maori pa, ancient gardens and rock art, the pictures in this book may, hopefully, generate a wider community interest in their preservation.

These pictures are generally indicative rather than definitive. The careful recording and analysis of sites is the job of an archaeologist; their cultural dimensions are increasingly reclaimed by Maori. Yet, without some common recognition of our past, these visual features of our shared landscape are at risk of being lost through neglect. Hence, the point of this album, to record features which helped determine the human character of our countryside, for broader appreciation.

Heritage of Aotearoa is not a guide book, though I hope it will help the observant eye to find further clues and locations of our past. While broadly travelled, its coverage has been arbitrarily proscribed by the places visited in the course of other work, or while holidaying. Often unfavourable weather made it impossible to photograph a particularly interesting feature but there should be sufficient 'representativeness' here to guide readers to make their own observations and enquiries. There are more detailed studies of regions and features listed at the end of this book.

My qualifications for making this record are practical not academic; an abiding curiosity has led to this and other portraits, intended as a sharing of enthusiasm for our common past and national heritage. Photography, for me, is a working tool in the making of a case for conservation, and for the enjoyment of our heritage. Next to direct experience, it allows the reader to make a personal observation; a personal judgement about what we may value.

Signs of the Past

THE STORY OF HUMAN SETTLEMENT in New Zealand is written in the landscape. The signs of European settlement are obvious, in forests cleared, swamps drained; nature obliterated by the burgeoning built environment. There are subtler signs in the landscape though, of a heritage reaching back much earlier, perhaps a thousand years, to the first settlement of Aotearoa by people. Often that 'writing' is little more than a shaded hollow on a hillside or a spill of broken shells from an eroding bank. Yet through careful observation it is possible to reconstruct from such remains how people once relied on land and sea for their sustenance.

Not even the radical changes of the past 200 years have quite wiped away the physical evidence of the first settlers of New Zealand. The sculptured forms of Maori pa or fortresses still crown many hills and scarps, particularly in the North Island. The subtler domestic signs of settlement — the garden walls, the orchards of karaka trees, fish traps and hunting camps — may still be detected in less disturbed places. Abandoned quarries, scattered with slivers of broken stone, mark places where people shaped their tools and weapons. In scattered caves, drawings in charcoal and red oxide record the early world of the Maori. This heritage of Aotearoa is the subject of these photographs.

These signs of the Maori past are representative only. They are a selection of portraits made in an endeavour to capture the peculiar quality given to our landscape by the early Maori. They are not intended as a guide; but simply as a visual aid to the recognition of such features, and a suggestion of their original function in material terms.

Information on specific pa and tribal heritage may be traced by non-Maori in the growing volume of tribal histories and guides. It is no longer fashionable for European New Zealanders and scholars to examine the specifics of Maori tradition and history. There is already argument aplenty about the work of recorders and interpreters of earlier years. Further there are the conflicting versions of what actually happened in Maori times, held within tribes but often varying from descendant family to family.

The distinguishing feature of New Zealand's 'pre-history' — and much of its fascination for many Europeans whose Stone Age was millenia ago — is that events of those times in Aotearoa are so recent as to be remembered not as artefacts but in living detail expressed through oral tradition. So analysis of the past is not popular with many Maori with whom it lives as part of the present, and a sign to the future.

The very recent nature of Maori 'pre-history' is reflected in the degree of remembered detail. The records of the land courts are full of varying versions of people's claims on the land through their rights of conquest and marriage. The family trees, which define claims and relate contemporary Maori in a continuum with their ancestors, are alive and specific, unlike most of the traditional stories which surround, for example, the British Stone Age fortresses such as Maiden Castle so strikingly like the Maori pa of New Zealand.

Memories of Maori times frequently survive in material terms too, in the collections of cultural objects and tools held in museums and by tribes and families. That history may be remembered in traditions surrounding, for example, a famous adze used in a remembered battle. Thus memories and traditions are re-inforced by physical tokens of the past.

STONE WALLS

A stone wall on Ahuahu (Great Mercury Island), site of very early Maori settlement in Aotearoa. While most Maori sites are marked today by banks and ditches formed from earth, Maori used stone in construction when this was readily available. Usually, stones gathered from the fields were stacked in walls marking out strips of horticultural land. Here, on Tamawera pa, house sites were retained and on occasions paved with stone.

The past (and the ancestors) live in the present people. In a context like this, the emergent Maori scholars of recent years have increasingly asked 'Who owns the past?' It is a question now asked all round the world, wherever indigenous people seek to protect their traditional knowledge, and heritage.

Partly in respect for this concern, this essay concerns itself, largely, with the material world; viewing the physical evidence of the past, as revealed in the landscape which is shared by all the various peoples of New Zealand. It is, indeed, the first in a series of volumes which examine signs of the impact of all people on the land; our historic places and landscapes. To attempt such a visual overview of our environment while ignoring signs of the Maori past would be to misrepresent the qualities of our human landscape. Some collective sensitivity to the signs of our past is a pre-requisite for protecting our various heritages. Ultimately the support of the people is required to legislate and fund for the protection of historic places.

The physical heritage of the Maori past is fragile. Most was never built to last; a fortress abandoned soon crumbled under the onslaught of storms, its banks eroded, its ditches filled by slippage. The timber posts in the defences out-lasted the nikau houses but fire and rot tumbled most within a century.

Some sites were occupied and re-occupied over time, as the tribal base shifted. The impacts are obvious on Auckland's volcanoes, still heavily marked by the terraces and fortifications of centuries. Yet traditions reveal they were occupied only intermittently as tribes changed location between them with the declining fertility of adjacent fields. Other pa, abandoned, perhaps after a defeat, may have become places of burial, fading memorials to a people wiped out by warfare or taken into slavery. A television news item about the desecration of a pa site by a Maori farmer is indicative of the narrowness of heritage and tribal affiliation. The pa was bull-dozed with the defence that it had no value to local Maori. Such a place may be sacred to one yet have little meaning to its conquerors.

Damage done to pa sites by farming and development is replicated at the sites of many other features. The extensive 'stone fields', the great Maori gardens of South Auckland about Mangere for example, have been largely and knowingly buried under industrial development, disturbed by public works, or quarried for stone. Seashore development has buried the camps of moa hunter and disturbed sacred places alike. In comparatively recent years road re-alignments and quarrying have destroyed ancient cave drawings from the limestone overhangs of North Otago and South Canterbury; others have been vandalised. Pine plantations have disguised the form of many early sites, just as the regenerating native bush has done naturally in other places.

Only in the comparatively recent past have features like pa and sacred places been protected in a raft of new environmental laws. Maori rights to be consulted as owners of this heritage now moderate the developmental race. But the changes come too late for hundreds of places where farms and forestry, roads and railways, power schemes and townships, have spread across historic fortifications and buried the signs of times past.

The Maori heritage of Aotearoa contributes much to the character of modern New Zealand. The landscape of the past is an aspect of this that other people can readily appreciate and value.

This album records some of the physical features that remain from earlier Maori times. It is largely a selection of readily recognisable shapes with some indication of their historic attributes and possible function. Hopefully, these pictures may readily serve as a key to features in the landscape worthy of protection. They are offered, in part, as a further contribution to the many good arguments for protecting the heritage of our past.

The First New Zealanders

The off-shore islands of northern New Zealand were among the earliest places settled by Maori. The islands are often similar in size to those of eastern Polynesia from which the Maori came. The coastal environment and warmth would have been more familiar to the voyagers than the cool forests of the mainland. This lagoon-like harbour on Ahuahu (an ancient name from Polynesia) lies on an isthmus between the two halves of Great Mercury Island, in the Bay of Plenty off Coromandel Peninsula. The beaches and fields nearby are littered with campsites, middens and the remains of stone-walled gardens, evidence of very early settlement. Sites on the adjacent mainland are among the most ancient recorded, perhaps dating from 1000 years ago.

THE FIRST NEW ZEALANDERS WERE POLYNESIANS. The remains of their camps and quarries, dating back around a thousand years, can still be found, particularly on the coast where food was plentiful and easier to harvest. The relics they left there in the sand dunes, their stone tools and weapons, ancient carvings and ornaments, resemble those of their Polynesian ancestors.

Such similarities in style and lifestyle are material evidence of the geographic origin of the first Maori, somewhere in Eastern Polynesia. Physique, language and legends also link those first settlers with a Polynesian island origin. Such factors, expanded on in tradition, are passed on in their descendants today. Modern ethnologists and anthropologists favour, as the most recent Maori homeland, somewhere in the Society Islands and/or the Marquesas, in Eastern Polynesia.

The more familiar Maori carving styles of recent centuries are different from those of other South Pacific islands, however. They are evidence of a developing culture, peculiar to New Zealand. So the first arrivals, the ancestral people before, are known as Archaic Maori, practised in the material culture of Eastern Polynesia. Their descendants, carving in a distinctive New Zealand style, are known as Classic Maori. That art is some of the physical evidence of the cultural changes which took place on the cooler shores of Aotearoa as the original Polynesian people adapted to a new land and became distinctively Maori.

While the evolution of Maori culture can be most easily traced through the comparative displays of tools and artefacts in our museums, the history of these changes can also be detected in the landscape. There were major and probably immediate changes made in encountering the new land. Aotearoa was colder than the tropic islands from whence the Maori came. It was also much larger and heavily forested, with different materials and foods to gather.

A Polynesian culture which, for example, included pigs and chickens in the diet, was immediately compromised for there were no such domestic animals in New Zealand. The islands of Aotearoa offered substitutes, however, including the giant and meaty moa bird among its rich birdlife, and the prolific bracken fern. The new people, who had been largely restricted, originally, to their small island group had once relied on fishing and horticulture for their food. In Aotearoa, the climate was generally too cold for their sub-tropical crops and there were few familiar plants, yet the settlers could wander more broadly among the islands and coasts. Moving with the seasons they could harvest the sea and the forest for an extensive range of plants, birds, insects and other food. These peripatetic Maori left no detectable signs of permanent settlements. The evidence of the many generations of Archaic Maori are found mainly in the form of seasonal campsites and artefacts left along the coast and pathways where they travelled.

Midden, or rubbish heap, left by early Maori in the sand dunes near Port Jackson, Coromandel Peninsula. The camp site was revealed when a storm shifted the sandhills and exposed the ancient site below. Blackened rocks are from fireplaces, some still in position near the top of the dune. Among the shells, lie the bones of birds and animals long gone from these shores. They included the bones of seals and of tuatara, a reptile from the age of dinosaurs which is now restricted to a few off-shore islands. Broken moa bones indicated where the early hunters had fed on carcases of this giant and now extinct bird. Analysis of shells and bones in such middens indicates what foods Maori relied on and also the early distribution of animals long-vanished from this coast.

On the conical hill, directly above the midden, are the distinctive horizontal markings which indicate the terraces of a later Maori fortress. The development of such Maori pa followed a cultural change from the peripatetic hunter-gatherer to a greater dependence on agriculture and the prospect of more permanent settlement.

SEASONAL CAMPS

The first Maori were a wandering people, moving from camp to camp with the seasons to take advantage of the changing food supply. Fishing camps and the cooking sites of the moa-hunters have been located near the mouths of many rivers. As a hunter-gatherer people they also visited the forests for birds, insects, and fruit. These activities left few physical marks on the land.

It is still possible to recognise some of camp sites on the surface of the land. At right, a rock shelter on Taranga (Hen Island), off the Whangarei coast contains surface evidence of Maori occupation. A scoop in the ground gathers water dripping from the rocks above — there is only one spring on the island. The round hammer stone could be used to open shells etc. A line of stones may have retained a protective brush wall. This campsite could be as recent as European times for Maori continued to make seasonal forays to hunting and fishing grounds despite the later development of agriculture and settlement in Classical times.

At left, the remains of fishing camps actually help to preserve the moving dunes at Mangawhai, in lower Northland. The fire stones and oily remains of cooking fish have congealed to form a capstone in the sand. Again, such sites may range in age over 1000 years. Archaeologists can date these camps by carbon-dating the organic material in the fireplaces and by the style of related artefacts.

Early tools chipped from basalt have a similar form to those made in Eastern Polynesia. Tools made at this quarry site at Opito Bay, Coromandel, have been found throughout the north proving early trade links. The Tahanga quarry is littered with flakes chipped from the basalt rocks by rounded hammer stones, some of which also lie broken on the quarry floor.

ARCHAIC STONE QUARRY

This quarry where tools were made in early times is high in the ranges near Nelson. Argillite from this area and adjacent D'Urville Island was a useful material. Again, examples of tools made from this rock have been found extensively in sites elsewhere in the country.

Trade between different areas appears to have been well developed by the twelfth century. The finding of tools from different regions has been widely used to construct theories about the spread of population and the extent of contact between early Maori groups.

A model by the Canterbury Museum shows how this quarry was worked. Toolmakers dropped large stones from the large rock on the bank onto the quarry floor. Suitably broken pieces were then chipped into the shape of tools, by striking with a harder stone which served as a hammer. Again, the ground is littered with chips struck off the core as the tool was shaped.

Granite provided hammers; sandstones served as smoothing grindstones. Maori refined the core of tools by hand rubbing them against harder rock, smoothing off rough edges, The smooth planes of Classic tools and weapons were created this way.

Greenstone from Te Wai Pounamu, was also traded throughout the country for making superior weapons and adornments.

Landmarks and Placenames

EXPLORER LANDMARK

Kahakaroa Big Dune at the North Head of the Hokianga Harbour in Northland.

The Hokianga is rich in traditions relating to the Polynesian explorer Kupe. He lived here awhile, after exploring the coasts of New Zealand and leaving his name on several land and seamarks along the way. One tradition has this as the departure point of Kupe when he left to return to his Hawaiki, or homeland in eastern Polynesia; this renders Hokianga as a literal placename, Te hoki anga o Kupe. Like many Maori placenames there are, however, other explanations and meanings.

THE EXPLORATORY VOYAGES OF THE MAORI across the Great Ocean of Kiwa to the islands of Aotearoa are enshrined in legend and tradition. The first explorers, men like Kupe, Toi and Whatonga, are celebrated in tribal traditions and their deeds recounted in the names of the places they visited. The earliest memories of migration tell of troubles in the ancestral Hawaiki, the setting out of exploratory canoes, the discovery and circumnavigation of New Zealand. Later tales tell of the settling of New Zealand by tribal canoes, sometimes direct from the Hawaiki, but often by journeys about the coast or through the forests.

Such migrations, often involved the conquering of other people along the way, usually eliminating their knowledge of an even earlier history. The remembered traditions of Maori tend to be the collective memories of those tribes which won the battles. In some places, however, such as Urewera, tribes merged combining their histories into particularly long associations with the land.

Those tribes who remember Kupe recall his naming places about the coast: Te Tangihanga o Kupe, the crying sound of Barretts Reef at the mouth of Port Nicholson, Wellington; Te Mana o Kupe ki Aotearoa, or Mana Island off Wellington, named in recognition of Kupe's achievement in discovery; Te Hoki anga o Kupe, the place from which Kupe left on his return journey to Hawaiki.

The Polynesian demi-god Maui fished up the land, using the blood of his own nose to bait a fish hook worked from the jawbone of his ancestress

Mahuika, goddess of fire. In Hawaiian myth he hauled up the island of Maui. In Aotearoa, the land came up in the form of Te Ika a Maui, or the North Island. This fish of Maui is shaped like a skate, with a mouth at Wellington, a hook at Cape Kidnappers (Te Matau o Maui), fins at East Cape and Cape Egmont, and the tail of the fish at Muriwhenua, land's end in the north. While Maui sought a priest to bless the new land his brothers began to chop it up. The tortured body of the fish, writhed, and wrinkled into mountains, breaking the perfect earth. So the traditions of the land explain its form.

The landmarks of Aotearoa reflect the associations of Maori with the land. Whangaparaoa, or the bay of whales just inside East Cape, was a landing place of several canoes, Arawa, Tainui, Mataatua. Large features of the coast have further names and connexions with the ocean-sailing canoes. At Whitianga on Coromandel, Tainui left an imprint of its sail against a cliff, Te Ra o Tainui. About the Auckland isthmus a whole raft of traditional names attach to places now buried by the city, yet recalling incidents on the voyage. Tainui then travelled down the west coast to tie up to a spreading pohutukawa in Kawhia Harbour. Its hull still lies buried just behind the beach of the small Maori settlement from which Tainui's people spread to occupy the inland hills and valleys of Waikato and the King Country.

The 'canoe' of Takitimu took a longer voyage. Landing some of its people in the Far North, it travelled then to Tauranga and on to the East Coast and Wairarapa. Over some 200-300 years it drifted (or was driven) south to the mountains of Southland where the Takitimu Range is an ancestor, some say the body of the canoe itself. Stories of Tamatea pokai whenua, the land strider, further associate the journey south with the features of the land. In some traditions, the name Kaikoura celebrates the fire at which Tamatea's crayfish was eaten — Te ahi kai koura a Tamatea Pokai Whenua.

As the landing places of the migratory canoes are remembered so too are

CANOE LANDING PLACES

These curious round rocks lying on the beach near Hampden in North Otago are said to be the cargo of the Arai-te-uru canoe which brought the sacred fire and sweet potato to these shores from the ancestral Hawaiki. Arai-te-uru had difficulty in navigating owing to an incorrectly recited prayer for safe passage. At length the listing canoe wrecked near Shag Point where its upturned hull can still be seen as a reef on Moeraki Beach. While the navigator, too, was turned to stone, the other people escaped ashore giving their names to many of the hills and landforms in this region of the South Island.

The cargo of the Aira-te-uru canoe was swept ashore to be preserved as the Moeraki Boulders. The smallest contained the tubers of the kumara or sweet potato. Larger stones were said to be the water calabashes while the largest were eel baskets. The woven baskets which contained the food may still be seen in the golden ridges which form a net around some of the more worn rocks.

other places where the ancestors wandered in search of new earth. Ngatoro i rangi of Arawa wandered as far inland as the volcanic country around Taupo where he called on his ancestors to send fire from Hawaiki to warm his body. When they obliged he sacrificed his slave Ngauruhoe, into the vent of that active volcano, in gratitude for its warmth.

Tribal boundaries are generally delineated by specific physical features. Sometimes a post of some sort serves as a boundary marker between tribes but more often it is a line of hills or a water boundary. Tribes may define themselves by acknowledging their major mountain and a water body among their progenitors. Thus:

Tongariro te maunga (Tongariro is the mountain)
Taupo te moana (Taupo is the sea)
Tuwharetoa te iwi (Tuwharetoa are the people)

The language of placenames often picks out the natural features: whanga for bay, maunga for mountain, roto for lake, wai for river; awa, a way. The names of ancestors associated with these places may often expand them into descriptive or allusive names, a sentence or more long.

Rangitoto is translated in one version as the 'isle of bloody skies'. The young volcano off Auckland bears a name that is both an ancient one from Hawaiki, and also a literal expression of its recent eruptions. Rangitoto is also an allusive contraction, from 'the day of the bleeding of Tama Te Kapua', captain of Arawa canoe, wounded in battle there or, more mundanely, cut about on the glass sharp scoria of the island. Placenames can reflect an often complicated relationship with land, spirit and ancestors.

The traditional place names of New Zealand are in themselves living evidence of another geography from an earlier time. Their attachment to the land adds a human dimension and a living tradition to many landmarks and to many more intimate landscapes too.

SPIRITUAL LANDMARK

Te Rerenga Wairua, the departing place of the spirits in the Far North of New Zealand. Spirits of the Maori dead journey here along Ninety Mile Beach and descend the ridge to a pohutukawa tree reaching over the sea. Here they enter the underworld for their last journey, joining their ancestors in Hawaikinui.

Stormy waters of the Tasman Sea meet the broad rollers of the South Pacific Ocean here at what is popularly known as Cape Reinga.

ANCESTORS & ANCESTRAL FEATURES

The ancestral mountains of the Maori have in some traditions a place in the very line of descent of their people. They are referred to in speeches as marker points in the relation of people to their land. They also have status, in some places, as living ancestors.

Tradition and legend often merge in the stories of significant mountains. Taranaki, (Mt Egmont) is regarded by some as an ancestor. Legend tells of a battle between the volcanoes of the central North Island, for the hand of Pihanga. The disappointed Taranaki strode away to the coast coming to rest against the bulk of the Pouakai Range. This unusually carved stone now stands by a marae near Puniho. Named Rauhoto Tapairu, the sacred figure is said to have guided Taranaki on his migration.

TRADITIONAL TRAILS AND PATHWAYS

Maori hunting and trading parties followed established routes through and beyond their home territories. The first European explorers often followed the war paths and trading routes traditionally used by Maori.

Ancient trails often combined walking routes with canoe voyages. Extended family parties travelled with the season to fishing, hunting and food-gathering grounds. The geography of their landscape included traditional campsites and sacred places. Seasonal progress through a region helped 'keep alive the fires' that warmed traditional links between people and land.

WAY MARKER

At left: the practice of a traveller making an offering for safe passage persists into the twenty-first century. A fresh twig has been left by this roadside marker in the Rotorua district. The stone is Te Turi o Hinengawari, the knee of the female tohunga who invested the stone with supernatural powers and placed it beside the main route to Waikato and the south. When passing strangers not knowing of the stone's powers failed to pay homage, Hinengawari roused the elements as warning to her people of the presence of strangers.

BROWNING PASS

Noti Raureka, an old greenstone trading route across the Southern Alps, was later used by gold-miners to reach the West Coast goldfields. The route passed up the broad Rakaia River, in the distance of this photograph, then followed up the Wilberforce (towards the camera). The pass involves a scramble up scree slopes to the little lake on the right before descending into the headwaters of the Arahura River in Westland.

Living off the Land

GATHERING KAIMOANA

The extensive coastal reefs and rivermouth lagoons provided a range of seafoods for the first settlers. Using techniques familiar from their home islands out in the Pacific, the first New Zealanders trolled lures and set nets for fish. The pattern of these early lures and barbless hooks are practically identical to those of the Pacific Islands they left; excepting the subtle changes in materials from pearl shell to paua, for example.

Extensive rock platforms like these at Tokomaru Bay, near East Cape, have been a valued source of kaimoana for centuries.

Shellfish and seaweeds garnered from the shore were another major type of food. Middens of rubbish indicate that as the moa birds became extinct in the south, hunters relied more on shellfish for their food. Harvesting the seashore remains an important aspect of Maori life. Special fishery regulations permit the taking of larger than usual quantities of restricted species, for important occasions organised by tribal elders.

THE FIRST NEW ZEALANDERS LIVED OFF THE LAND and adjoining sea. The apparent harshness of this environment is moderated by its riches and diversity. The islands of Aotearoa were colder than those to the north but they were much larger and had many more species of plants and animals. The Polynesians adapted what they knew of the Pacific islands to make a living off this new land.

There were myriad birds both along the shore and inland. The reefs and estuaries were rich in fish and molluscs. The swamps, rivers and lakes were further habitat for birds and fish and freshwater molluscs. The forests provided not only habitat for birds but materials for shelter, plants for medicines, a seasonal range of berries and other fruits, insects to eat, fibres to weave and bind.

A people who had lived off taro, kumara, coconut and breadfruit, complemented by fish from the lagoon immediately adapted to fishing the shores and eating the produce of the new land. Sometimes they gave a tropical name to a similar-looking species, though it might not present the same qualities or place in their new economy. Thus the kawakawa resembles the kava, active ingredient in Fiji of a chiefly drink, and in New Zealand having much the same mild effect as its Pacific relative.

The first settlers found in the forests a treasure house of food and materials. The ancient Polynesian legends attached themselves to a new range of plants and wild creatures. The gods remained: Tane over the forests, Tangaroa over the oceans, Haumia over the wild foods and Rongo over the planted ones.

The winds of Tamatea still blew and the spirit of Tu, the war-like man, still stood against the elements.

In the new land, the traditional deeds of the demi-gods were given new meanings, relative to the different plants and birds now discovered. Maui the trickster still stole fire from his ancestor Mahuika but here he placed it in the twigs of New Zealand shrubs; here Maori made fire with hardwood friction drills of kaikomako, spun on shreds of the softer whau. Maui's deeds in fishing up the land extend in various Polynesian versions, from the northern Pacific and the island of Maui in Hawaii, to Aotearoa where he fished up the North Island.

Rata who built a canoe in the forest without first seeking the blessing of Tane was corrected with the re-erection of his felled tree by a party of New Zealand birds and forest creatures. The spiritual rules of living with the land became established in Aotearoa and developed with its special nature.

The traditions and practices connected with the harvest of nature are still recalled in certain parts of New Zealand. While a fraction of this knowledge was captured in the books of European observers, much remains the exclusive knowledge and propery of tribal elders. The expression may vary from a simple but all-encompassing imperative 'Don't cheek the sea' to a heartfelt and complex concern over the abuse of waters; the damage done to spiritual health through such practices as diversion, abstraction and pollution. Consequently, a general respect for the forest and the sea has been enshrined in recent legislation protecting the land and its waters. Many non-Maori New Zealanders also share, albeit from a different perspective, a desire to protect native wildlife and species, to clean-up waterways and stop polluting the air and sea. Such protective urges stem from a groundswell of public opinion which is the modern expression of an ancient respect for the earth, common to many cultures, but which is particularly so for Maori in Aotearoa.

VALUABLE PLANTS

Early Polynesian settlers swiftly adapted the skills and knowledge of their Pacific homelands to the resources available in Aotearoa. Among the tropical plants they introduced was the paper mulberry or aute. This shrub is the source of bark from which tapa cloth is made, an important material in the tropical Pacific.

In the colder climate of New Zealand, the paper mulberry languished, and has since become extinct in the wild. Maori then used flax as a basic fabric for weaving textiles.

The whau (at right) is a native of warmer New Zealand and a close relative of paper mulberry. While unsuitable for making cloth, its very light wood was used for the manufacture of fishing floats. As a soft dry material, shredded whau was also used to make fire. A smouldering fire was started by friction generated by a drill made from a harder timber, notably kaikomako.

VALUABLE FIBRES

Harakeke or flax (*Phormium* spp.) was invaluable to a people deprived of their traditional textiles by the colder climate of New Zealand. Flax fibres were stripped and dried for the making of clothing, bags and mats. In finer work, flax formed the framework into which dogskin and feathers were incorporated. Flax also provided material for netting and rope. Often grown in plantations (above) it complemented wild materials such as toetoe, pingao (at right), nikau palm leaves, and various lianes.

The berries of karaka were among those gathered in the wild. The highly poisonous kernels were baked and soaked for many days, to make them safe to eat. Generally a coastal tree, karaka sometimes occurs in groves inland where it was probably planted beside a settlement to be more readily available. These trees grow on the slopes of Pouerua, near Bay of Islands, and adjacent to the defended summit.

Moa Hunters and Wild Foods

THE FIRES OF TAMATEA

Around the fourteenth century, great fires burnt the forested plains and high country of Canterbury and Otago. Burnt totara logs from these conflagrations still litter some of the hills.

The fires are sometimes named for the explorer Tamatea whenua pokai, who is said to have travelled this land burning the natural cover as he went. Such fires are believed to have chased the flightless moa birds into the open where they could be more easily captured..

Here, on the Rock and Pillar Range of Central Otago, is a tiny remnant of the old forest type preserved deep in a cold and south-facing gully. The species of plants that survive here were once typical of the green cover of the surrounding hills. Climate change, due in large part to the clearance of the forest, has been blamed for the failure of trees to regrow on the exposed country.

MAORI CAME TO A LAND so isolated from the continents that it had no land animals, no wild animals, save three species of tiny bats. There were seals and whales about the coast but everywhere the prolific birdlife flourished in the absence of predators, excepting their own kind. So numbers of large-boned flightless birds survived, previously unthreatened by ground-dwelling enemies. Maori hunters were their first.

Maori also had dogs, brought from eastern Polynesia. The animals were used to hunt and their flesh and skins were also useful. The Polynesian rat, *Rattus exulans* was another mammal introduced by Maori. It shortly over-ran the bush. Dogs, rats and people had a tremendous impact on the species of birds which had evolved in their absence. Within the period of Maori settlement 33 species of bird became extinct.

Greatest among them were the moa, a group of 12 or 14 species (scientists are still deciding their number) ranging from a small bush moa, standing about knee high to its hunter, to the biggest bird ever known to exist in modern times, the Giant Moa reaching more than four metres tall. So dependent were some Maori on its flesh that they are known still as the Moa-hunters. Their middens of waste bones and the extensive butchering areas about the mouths of southern rivers, have been excavated to reveal that the moa-hunters were among those first settlers in New Zealand. Their artefacts and burials have helped establish the nature and extent of early settlement, helping to define the lifestyle of the Archaic Maori.

Some have been blamed not only for the extinction of the moa but also for the initial burning of the South Island forests to make hunting easier. Blackened stumps and trunks of long gone totara forests about Canterbury and Otago are given as physical evidence of the traditionally remembered 'fires of Tamatea' which, raging in the fourteenth century, cleared many of the foothills and much of the plains. Some sensitive Maori now blame these fires on natural disasters, ignition by lightning perhaps, but the fact remains that the great forests perished not long before the moa.

In other districts bush was burned to encourage the growth of bracken fern. Extensive areas of this tough-springing fern dominated the landscape particularly where population was heavy, about the Bay of Islands and the isthmus of Auckland, for recorded examples. Maori in many places relied on fern root as a staple food, pounding it into a flour from which cakes could be baked.

Such management of wild foods extended to managing plantations of other native plants to produce food and materials. Flax was an obvious crop, encouraged in damp beds to produce ropes and materials for weaving: its bye-products included a cure for constipation and material for the making of bandages, while the flower stalks could be bound in bundles to provide flotation, as a personal swiming aid or bound together in the form of rafts.

The karaka was another plantation tree. Its poisonous kernels are contained in luscious-looking yellow berries. Maori had a way of leaching the poison from the kernels and making meal from it. There are nevertheless horrific stories of children in paroxysms being buried to their neck in sand after eating the poisonous berries. Ranks of karaka trees, particularly adjacent to old pa sites are often visual evidence of an early orchard.

BRACKEN FERN

The ryhzomes of this hardy fern were the source of a staple food from earliest times. A flour-like meal was extracted using fern root beaters, almost identical with the implements used in such places as Samoa, Tonga and the Cook islands. So dependent on fern root did Maori become that large areas of forest were burnt off to produce it. The bracken fern grew in open conditions replacing the forests in large parts of Hawkes Bay and the north.

Only the introduction of the kumara and later the potato freed Maori from reliance on fern root meal. It remained a staple food, however, generally available in times of need. Travelling parties could dig up the fern root and produce meal for baking cakes or eating uncooked while on the trail.

CABBAGE TREES

The root and young shoots of various cabbage trees *Cordyline* spp. were a valued source of sugar. In the south of New Zealand, in particular, Maori made seasonal camps at places where the trees grew in groves. Young trees about 1.3 metres high were favoured. Earth ovens lined with stones, where the roots were steam cooked, can still be located in parts of Otago. Leaves from the tree provided another source of fibre, used for cooking baskets.

Rock Drawings and Carvings

ROCK SHELTERS

The Maerewhenua rock shelter near Duntroon overlooks the Waitaki Valley in North Otago. This was the route inland for Maori hunting parties. Sites like this were visited seasonally for hundreds of years. They provided good, warm shelter for the traveller. The back wall of this shelter is extensively decorated (samples page 50-51).

Dates for Maori rock art are difficult to establish with ages of up to 500 years claimed for some. The drawings include flightless moa and extinct eagle suggesting an early date. Others, by dint of their subject material, date from European times. Seasonal hunting on traditional grounds continued well into the nineteenth century.

IN THE HILL-COUNTRY CAVES of the South Island, fading drawings on the rock record the experience of early Maori who once hunted here. Giant birds in flight and earth-bound moa are among the symbols marked onto the walls of limestone shelters in rudimentary charcoal or red earth. Canoes and rafts, dogs, seals, eels, and fish hint at the world picture of the early travellers. Mythical beasts such as bird men and taniwha reflect their beliefs. No one is certain of their age or purpose.

The cave drawings of Canterbury and Otago have been suggested as being some record or reflection on the land by a people with no alternative in written language. Equally the symbols may be seen as religious tokens or fancied charms for good or against evil. Some believe these pictures date to the fourteenth century or before when moa roamed these hills. Many are attributed to Waitaha, ancient people of the south, preceding the successive invasions of Kati-mamoe and later Ngai Tahu and still claimants for the spiritual ownership of the high country. It has been suggested by scholars that some drawings may date back over several hundred years.

Among the symbols recorded are fresher ones, however, including the sailing ships of Europeans, a horse and Maori names spelt out in the elegant calligraphy taught by the nineteenth-century missions.

The materials used in this cave art are simple. The black is charcoal, sometimes mixed with bird or seal oil which leads to greater penetration of the rock face. The red is a naturally occurring red oxide, a colour sacred to Maori. The source material is the softish rock called haematite which can be crushed and reformed into crayons, sometimes again with a binding of oil. This kokowai can still be found in middens of waste, about ancient Maori settlements. Early records tell of Maori wearing this colour smeared on their bodies. A yellow colour in some drawings is the product of scraping away the encrusted surface of the rock to reveal the lemon-coloured native limestone beneath.

Some artists made use only of colour to create their designs while others incorporated the wall itself into their drawings, creating negative effects of raw stone within their work. The scale of these drawings varies from a modest animal or human form about 50 centimetres across to taniwha and other monsters which may run for three or four metres across the rock.

Many drawings have been defaced in the past century. Farm animals, sheltering sheep and goats, have rubbed many away. Others have been vandalised by visitors or drawn over. Significant cave drawings have been drowned by hydro lakes or converted to road metal and fill. Some have simply faded through time and it now requires a skilled examination of the rock face to detect them. Often the clearest photographs are of paintings which have been 'touched up' by recordists, an action which at once makes the image clearer and destroys its integrity. Sadly, a journey to observe such drawings using, say, a record of even 20 years ago leads so often to disappointment, with the drawings defaced, damaged or destroyed in the interim.

Rock drawings are not restricted to the south: there are red ones beside Lake Tarawera in the Rotorua district and more in cave shelters in the King Country. They are found in greatest number, however, in the south, about limestone country from North Canterbury to Central Otago.

The drawings on walls and ceilings are generally in shallow caves or overhangs, mere shelters below an over-bearing outcrop or limestone bluff. Many give a distant view across a plain or valley where game once wandered. The usefulness and security of such shelters, to the traveller, is obvious as the long cold evening closes across the downs. The floor of such caves is usually a midden of oily black fats and fireplaces, left by the passage of hunting parties through the centuries. Most have since been sealed with a century or more of stock manure left by sheltering animals.

Stone carvings are less frequently found but are none-the-less spectacular. Those in the forests of Kaingaroa, in the central North Island, are carved from soft volcanic rock, again in an overhanging rock shelter. Their style includes carving in the rock itself, and raised images where the surrounding stone has been carved away to leave the canoe symbols in relief.

Decorated stones have been recorded from Taranaki, the Waikato coastline and Mayor Island. The carved figure of Matuatonga, on Mokoia Island, Rotorua, is sculpted from soft volcanic stone, a super-human-sized figure made in the traditional image of the smaller carved figures placed among kumara crops.

Another perspective of the Maerewhenua rock shelter, high on a limestone bluff above the valley of the Waitaki River, near Duntroon. Maori rock art occurs at several points along this inland route, though several sites were drowned by the rising waters of Lake Benmore, built to generate electricity further upstream.

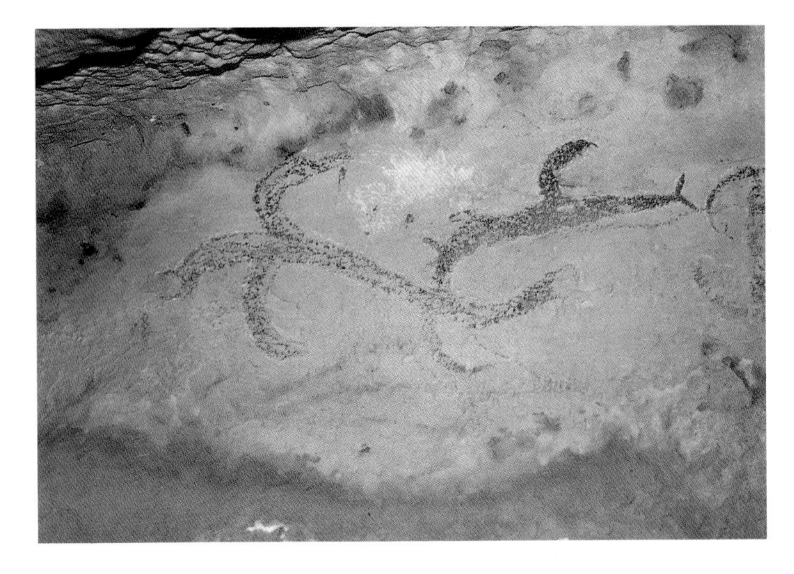

NORTH OTAGO ROCK DRAWINGS

An extensive display of Maori rock art seen at the Maerewhenua site, near Duntroon, in the Waitaki River valley.

Largely executed in charcoal, these drawings include monsters and canoes. Their fading detail is typical of a well preserved site.

The details pictured at left can be identified within the broader picture at right. This, in turn, is just part of a long gallery now protected from sheltering stock by a wire fence. The lighter areas around the central canoe figures are where collectors in the early nineteenth century removed some of the more interesting drawings.

The view from the Maerewhenua rock shelter, commanding the Waitaki Valley, is shown on page 46.

Old drawings in red ochre, or haematite, a colour sacred to Maori. These drawings are in a shelter by the roadside in the Waitaki Valley at a locality called Takiroa. The symbols above are enigmatic and the ghosts of earlier images also confuse. The taniwha at left is still distinct despite the number of livestock which may have sheltered here over the years. The pincers of the taniwha are about to close on its prey.

A typical rock art site near Raincliff in South Canterbury. Limestone overhangs, or rock shelters, are the usual site of Maori rock drawings. The soft rock absorbs the charcoal and red oxide materials used by early artists, while the limestone itself can be incorporated into the designs. The dry cave air protects them.

These Maori cave drawings, at Timpendean on the Weka Pass in North Canterbury, were retouched with housepaint in the early 1900s. The subtlety of the originals has been destroyed. The quality of the originals may just be glimpsed in the faint images which survive between the repainted images (right).

Rock drawings are rare in the North Island. These drawings in the western King Country are also made on limestone and are similar in form to those found in the South Island. Rock carving is a more frequent form of art in the north where designs are occasionally found inscribed in soft volcanic stone.

At left, a closer detail of a figure painted on the cliff face at the King Country site. This is on private land.

At right: Rock drawings beside Lake Tarawera in the Rotorua district of the North Island. The drawings were for some time under the lake when its outlet was blocked during the volcanic eruption of Mount Tarawera in 1886. The drawings in red ochre resemble canoes. Canoe symbols, carved in stone, are also a motif at several sites in the upper Waikato and Rotorua regions.

Rock carvings in a cave in Kaingaroa Forest in the Rotorua region. The major features consist of 24 canoes carved in the soft volcanic material making up the back wall of a rock overhang. In the examples above the canoes have been carved in relief, with a series of koru carved into the side of the lower one. At right, the canoe outlines are carved into the soft rock.

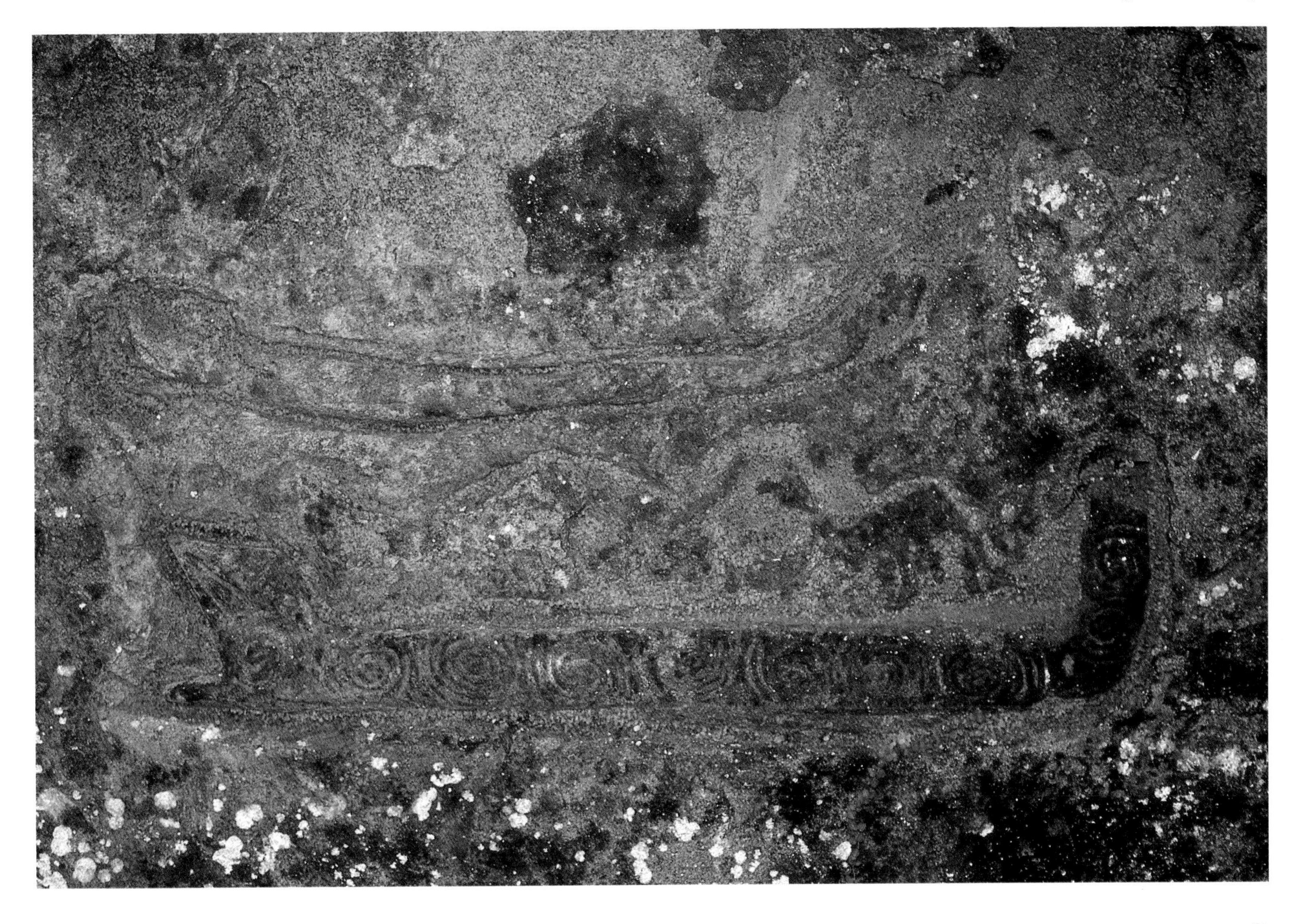

Myths of the Moriori

THE NAME OF MORIORI IS PERHAPS THE MOST CONFUSED in the popular beliefs about the early settlement of New Zealand. The Maori practice of taking land by conquest gave credence to the myth of a primitive early people who were here before the Maori. According to this theory, sophisticated Maori tribes, borne to Aotearoa aboard a great fleet of canoes, over-ran a simple and primitive people who were the original occupants of the land.

The theory was a popular one in the nineteenth and early twentieth century when, (it is now said), the waves of conquest upon conquest helped justify the subsequent British invasion of Maori land. More likely in those simpler times, however, the tale of a previous and primitive people was a convenient way of explaining the puzzling differences between the Classic Maori culture encountered by the first European settlers and the obvious evidence of a hunter-gatherer culture now known as Archaic Maori.

For nineteenth-century scientists, many of whom believed literally that God created the Earth in seven days, the mysteries of social and cultural evolution were hard to explore. Some came to the conclusion that a race of small, dark people, probably of Melanesian origin had settled New Zealand before the Maori. Others found in the Bible references to the lost tribes of Israel and gave them an origin among wandering Jews. Others suggested Aryan origins, and made much of the blonde and red-headed people in the Urewera region, a place incidentally which had retained a tradition of descending both from invaders and original inhabitants.

In exploring these mysteries, scholars, both European and Maori, concocted a possible history which involved a primitive Moriori or Maruiwi people being defeated by a migration of canoes from Polynesia about 1340.

Many of today's tribes do descend from the people of the great canoes but scholars, such as David Simmons, have shown by examining genealogies that not all these canoes came together in one all-conquering fleet. Traditions of the plants and animals carried aboard these canoes also suggest that, for some at least, the journey to their present lands from Hawaiki, may have begun in some northern part of New Zealand, not eastern Polynesia. Maori traditions record in excess of 63 founding canoes, not the simple seven of the Great Fleet. This number is swollen in some cases by the insistence of early land courts that all Maori tribes must have a founding canoe or they would not be here. Yet among Ngati Porou there is a belief they have always been here. Other tribes tell of migrations, within New Zealand, by land rather than by sea.

Whatever the origins of today's tribes, in terms of an original homeland, they all share the same basic culture; a culture which has been demonstrated as developing in New Zealand from a common ancestry in Eastern Polynesia. The original people, according to the material evidence of their tools and cultural practices, were Polynesians.

The tribal nations encountered by the first Europeans were those which had evolved through successive conquests over the centuries. The traditions of the conquered may well have been destroyed in the interests of the conquerors but the physical records they left are extensive and, in some cases, where chiefly lines were married rather than destroyed, some early traditions survive alongside those of the present 'people of the land'.

The name of Moriori is now ascribed to another culture which evolved from Eastern Polynesia, separately from Maori, on the Chatham islands.

Carvings in limestone, in a seaside cave on the main Chatham Island. These petroglyphs are said to resemble bird and seal figures. They date from the times of the original settlers of the Chatham islands, the Moriori people, another culture of eastern Polynesian origin, distinct from Maori in language and values.

Much was made earlier in the twentieth century of the demise of these people, the impressive image of the massive Tommy Solomon being widely published with the caption, the 'Last of the Moriori'. Solomon died, weighing 190 kilograms, in 1933 but his relatives, albeit inter-married with Maori or European, live on. In the 1970s a revival of Moriori culture saw people from the island and the mainland reclaiming their history and their own Polynesian language from their Maori conquerors.

The Chatham Islands, some 1000 kilometres to the east of New Zealand, have a different history from the mainland and the Moriori people evolved their own culture there in isolation. The islands were settled from New Zealand but long enough ago for their original language to have developed its own vocabulary and dialect, distinct from Maori in sound and expression. Their traditions tell of a simpler lifestyle, more peaceable than Maori, living off the land largely through hunting, fishing and gathering from the forest and shore. When displaced Maori tribes in the Wellington area commandeered a European ship in 1835 they sailed two parties to the islands and conquered the Moriori. Raped, killed or enslaved, the Moriori were in the classic situation of a people conquered, in danger of losing their bloodlines and their past, submerged beneath the culture of their conquerors.

Yet this latest of Maori migrations was to encounter the introduction of British law, arresting the total annihilation of Moriori culture. The Chatham islands were handed from the care of the convict colony of Van Dieman's Land (now Tasmania) into the governorship of New Zealand in 1842, some two years after the introduction of British rule through the signing of the Treaty of Waitangi.

The Maori occupation was marked by bitter tribal warfare. Then, after a disastrous tidal wave in 1868, many Maori returned to the mainland, rejoining their ancestral tribes, centred on Taranaki. Again, some later returned to 'Wharekauri'. The nature of Maori conquest on the Chathams, its annexation after the Treaty was signed and the survival of Moriori culture, have consequently created a divided community. Faced with the recent possibility of tremendous wealth through the allocation of fishing rights to the surrounding waters of the islands, through the Maori Fisheries Commission, Chatham Islanders are at odds over who the owners will be. Conquerors and original settlers, now inter-married but divided by family histories, are arguing over their comparative rights.

The Moriori heritage is very much alive though the language has to be relearned. The archaeological evidence of the island provides another sequence of Polynesian materials, tools and other artefacts which firmly identify the Moriori as another culture descendant from the eastern Polynesians. For the visitor today the material evidence is most obvious in the carvings from the past: the fading dendroglyphs or figure carvings in the bark of ancient kopi trees, (known on the mainland as karaka); and petroglyphs, or stone carvings, in a limestone overhang, overlooking the Te Whanga lagoon on Chatham Island.

DENDROGLYPHS

Wood carvings, or dendroglyphs, carved by Moriori people of the Chatham Islands. The abstract figures are carved in the bark of the kopi tree, the Moriori name for karaka. Groves of these trees were once widespread on the island and the dendroglyphs numbered in their thousands. Grazing cattle have destroyed most of the original kopi forest (as pictured above) and most of the figures fell with the bark of the dying trees. The dendroglyphs on these trees survive in a fenced reserve at the end of the old airport at Haupupu.

The Maori Gardeners

THE POLYNESIANS WHO FIRST SETTLED New Zealand, did not neglect their remembered traditions of gardening and in a few warm corners of Aotearoa succeeded in planting kumara (sweet potatoes), the tropical yams, and gourds, taro in wet patches, the paper mulberry and the tropical cabbage tree. Not all such crops survived and certainly they would not grow much beyond the shores of the farthest, northern islands and those coasts where sub-tropical micro-climates protected the viability of their seeds. While they still fished the oceans and gathered wild birds and plants in season, these gardeners were not wholly dependent on the wilderness for their survival; unlike those who hunted, fished and gathered food in colder climates.

The signs of Maori gardening can still be traced in some places where subsequent farmers have left the Polynesian stone walls in their fields.

Lines of stones have been declared, arguably, to be family boundaries, as they still are in some parts of Polynesia. Others have pointed out the value of stone walls in reducing wind and creating shelter for planting out kumara. Piles of stones, by contrast, create a micro-climate, the stones retaining enough warmth to bring the tropical yam and gourd to fruit. These gourds, known as hue, were particularly useful as water vessels in a society which had lost the knowledge of how to make pottery. Otherwise containers were carved in wood, made of bark, or sometimes the hard leaf-heel of a nikau palm, the bladders of kelp, or plaited from flax.

Taro is a widespread root vegetable of tropical lands. It will grow in warmer New Zealand, a source of starch, and is still a feature of some northern

GARDEN WALLS

Signs of early gardens at Ihumatao on the shores of Manukau Harbour, Auckland. A naturally rocky terrain has been cleared into sheltered areas with rocks stacked into protective walls. Shelter and radiant heat from the rocks creates a micro-climate in which sub-tropical crops could be grown.

creekbeds. Like the kumara and the yam, the modern taro is a specially bred successor to the wild strains first brought to these shores.

Most of the original Polynesian vegetables have become extinct in the past 200 years as new strains were introduced from other countries. A Maori trust at Mangere in south Auckland has obtained some stocks of earlier strains, gathered in New Zealand but held in a collection in Japan for many years. The trust seeks to re-establish the traditional strains in a demonstration garden by the mountain.

According to tradition, the tropical paper mulberry, known as aute, was introduced to New Zealand by the canoe voyagers. From it Polynesian islanders still make the papery fabric known as tapa cloth. In Aotearoa the plant grew only in a few favoured corners. Maori used flax, dog hair, and bird and seal skins, as substitutes for the tapa fabric.

GARDENS OF STONE

Stone piles, like those in this paddock inland from the Bay of Islands, are a clue to the location of early Maori gardens. The straight-line walls are the product of European farming, built from volcanic rocks gathered up about the foot of Pouerua mountain. The scattered piles are where Maori grew their tropical crops such as gourds (hue) and yams. The piles of dark stones readily absorbed and stored the heat of the sun. This increased warmth made it possible for tropical plants, introduced by Maori, to thrive in the colder climates of Aotearoa.

Early morning light illuminates the grass-covered stone piles of Maori agriculture on the Taiamai Plain inland from the Bay of Islands. Earth was mixed in with the piles to make a seed bed.

Maori settlement on Great Mercury Island (Ahuahu), east of Coromandel Peninsula, dates back 800 years or more. These extensive field systems are adjacent to the great stone-terraced Tamawera Pa on the rounded headland. Walls like this recall Polynesian field systems. The stone walls create a micro-climate, retaining heat and sheltering kumara crops from the salt winds.

Extensive stone fields in the Waipoua Forest in Northland have been over-planted with pine plantations. An understorey of native shrubs now further confuses the outlines and extent of a once-great settlement. Stone piles, hearth stones and other structures can still be traced in the forest.

The Kumara

THE RETURN TO HAWAIKI

Traditions of the migrants from Polynesia often include a special return journey 'home', to Hawaiki, to obtain stock of the kumara or sweet potato. The island of Ahuahu, or Great Mercury in the Bay of Plenty has been postulated as one such Hawaiki.

In Aotearoa, the plant grows at the southern limit of its range, so it survives only in a few warm corners without special care. Ahuahu is one of the few places where it grows naturally. Tradition tells of a voyage back to fetch kumara and the sailing directions match those for reaching Ahuahu, itself an ancient name for Hawaiki. At the foot of the great cliff Parinuitera the voyagers find kumara growing and return with stocks to Aotearoa.

The island's great white cliffs are a beacon to approaching canoes from the Pacific. It would seem a likely place for very early settlement, and as an island more welcoming than the forested mainland. It has been suggested that Ahuahu is but one link in a chain of Hawaiki stretching back into the migratory past of the peoples of the Pacific.

UNDERSTANDABLY THE SETTLERS, who were restricted to what they could gather from the land and sea, would covet the crops of kumara. Maori traditions contain many allusions to this staple crop. *Ipomea batatas* is also the sweet potato of Asia and originally the Americas. In New Zealand Maori it has more than 80 names, each descriptive of a type or quality or reflecting a locality. So its importance in the horticultural economy is suggested in material terms.

Unfortunately, for the first settlers, kumara will not flourish in frosty places. Tribes who could grow the crop were indeed fortunate for, while they must still wander in pursuit of seasonal foods, taking birds or fish or berries, they had in the kumara staple food for the short cold days of winter.

A successful crop of kumara, however, placed some major restraints on people who would otherwise be on the move in search of food. Kumara takes several months to cultivate. It requires a prepared field and care through its growth. Such sedentary occupation requires permanant settlement. A successful crop allows for this, for it creates a store of food, both difficult to move, but easy to rely on. It also provokes the covetousness of neighbouring people. Then, not only is a more permanent settlement required, but so also must its defence be attended to. The fortified Maori pa with its kumara storage pits and defensive ditches and walls was a practical and necessary response.

The traditions of several tribes recount a journey back to an ancestral Hawaiki to obtain the kumara for their gardens. Some take this as evidence that Maori people returned to some previous home in the tropical Pacific, to obtain their seed stocks. Others argue that such journeys might be more local, northwards, perhaps to an earlier-settled island, an Hawaiki about the New Zealand coast, where mild conditions allowed the kumara to survive.

In any event the successful gardening and storage of kumara requires special treatment in New Zealand, for the far north swiftly merges into the southern limit of growth for this tropical plant. It was the discovery of how to store this kumara through the frosty periods which changed Maori life. The not-so-humble kumara is credited with triggering a social revolution which produced a new culture based on permanent settlement. Its marks on the land include the significant heritage of Maori pa or fortresses and the curious holes in the ground which were once used to store kumara.

These kumara pits, usually about the ground dimension of a small shed, are the remains of sunken houses in which the vegetable was stored. Here, underground, the temperature was warmer than in the raised storehouses. In winter the critical temperature stayed above the 10 degrees Celsius required to keep the seed stock alive.

The mighty fortresses, the pa sites which still dominate the landscape, are evidence of this developing technology. While Maori became less dependent on wild foods, they were now tied, seasonally at least, to their gardens. The formation of these more or less permanent villages created a situation requiring defence for its residents and protection for their coveted crops.

More-abundant food had positive effects too. Stores of food lifted the living above hand-to-mouth survival to allow a modicum of leisure. This in turn made possible a development of the arts, most evident now in the intricate carving of Classic Maori culture. So a humble vegetable is credited with helping transform the Eastern Polynesians into New Zealand Maori.

KUMARA PITS

A complex of kumara pits within the confines of a formerly fortified Maori pa near Whitianga, Coromandel Peninsula. The hilltop pa is surrounded by terraces and these kumara pits have been dug into an artificially flattened spur. The area is surrounded by a steep escarpment which was probably also topped by a palisade of logs. The highly valued kumara could be stored here, protected by the surrounding fortress, and readily available to feed the defenders of the pa should they come under attack.

Kumara pits were basically sunken huts where the sweet potato was kept viable through the cold of winter. Generally about 1.5 metres deep, many have been filled nearly to the brim with debris since abandonment. Originally the kumara pits were roofed with nikau leaves or totara bark and had a low door for access to the store at one end.

Occasionally Maori house sites can be confused with storage pits; this is where the house has been dug some way into the earth to provide extra warmth to the occupants.

KUMARA STORES

Other forms of kumara storage included the bell-shaped pit and the cave.

The bell pit (near right) has a narrow opening but opens out underground like a bell to contain kumara. A wooden lid kept out pests and the weather. The natural warmth underground helped keep the kumara viable. This bell pit is one of several within the confines of Ruapekapeka Pa, near the Bay of Islands.

The rua or cave (far right) was usually excavated in soft material like pumice. Inside, the cave opened up like a bell on its side. The suggestion of an engraved line, around the entrance, marks where a door was fitted to keep out rats and dogs. Rua were usually dug into the inner banks of fortified pa and accessed from the defensive ditch. This saved space where flat ground was at a premium within the pa. This is one of a series of rua in the banks of a defended hillside at Lake Okataina, near Rotorua.

Occasionally much larger pits were dug to keep very large quantities of kumara. These may have been sufficient to feed a beleagured garrison or provide for a great ceremonial occasion. This pit (at left) is part of the extensive pa which covers Maungawhau (Mt Eden) in Auckland.

The pit is perched near the rim of the volcanic crater. There are normal-sized pits about the rim and more on the level area beyond, on what was once the top of the pa.

MATUATONGA

The giant figure of Matuatonga (left) still guards the ancient kumara fields on Mokoia Island in Lake Rotorua. Stone-carving is an unusual medium in Maori art, certainly on this scale. Matuatonga is carved from pumice in a form similar to much smaller carvings formerly placed in gardens to protect the crops. Generally they represent the god Rongo, the traditional protector of planted crops.

Rocks, carvings, and other inanimate objects, could become the temporary resting place of a spirit, or embody the mauri or life force, in this case of the kumara crop. The rocks above, on Mangere mountain in Auckland, stand on a high point on the rim of the volcano. Such an assemblage of stones could serve as an 'altar' for religious observance or, again, act as a resting place for spirits or life force.

Maori Pa and Settlements

LIVING TERRACES

Terraced pa site on the upper slopes of Maungakiekie, or One Tree Hill, in Auckland. Terraces dug into the volcanic cones were the sites of houses and storage pits. Higher up the cone, ditches and banks, once surmounted by palisades, protect the highest points. (Pictured on page 98-99).

THE BUILDING OF MAORI PA OR FORTRESSES is generally believed to date from the time when people began to rely on kumara gardens for much of their staple food. The pa was built as a fortress to defend the people and their crops. The sweet potato needed to be cared for, while it grew, so people lived beside the gardens. When the crop was gathered in the autumn, then it had to be defended from those who would steal it. Kumara were often stored in pits dug within the protective palisades of the pa.

The fortified hills and headlands of Aotearoa are still conspicuous features of the landscape. Especially when the sun is low, casting its shadows across the land, the unnaturally straight lines of banks and ditch can often be traced, disturbing the natural curves of the earth. Some pa have survived for centuries, through repeated use; others are the fast-fading relics of the nineteenth century, when Maori often dug only shallow trenches and rifle pits to fight a new kind of war; using guns in place of the traditional weapons of hand-to-hand fighting.

The essential purpose of the Maori pa was defence, a defended position dug into the land and topped with palisades to resist the enemy. Often defenders lived outside the pa, in more convenient villages, withdrawing to their citadel when attacked. The sites varied, according to local topography. A headland could be defended by cutting a trench across its neck and piling the earth into banks on which the palisades were raised. The natural fall of surrounding cliffs and bluffs largely protected the seaward sides of the headland pa from attack. Another method was to surround a hill or high point with successive ditches and banks, defending it from all comers. Ridge tops could

The terraces of an ancient Maori pa near Whitianga are revealed by low sunlight. Banks and terrace edges once carried palisades of logs. A break through the bank (opposite page, foreground) may mark a narrow entry. Gates were often overlooked by a high platform from which defenders threw down stones.

also be defended by cutting across them with ditches and banks to create a section of ridge defended at either end by palisades and along the sides by natural bluffs of steep-falling land. On flatter sites, fortresses could be built by surrounding an area of land with a ditch and bank, raising the palisades above. Some pa were built on islands in lakes or swamps and were thus protected by a natural moat. Off-shore islets served as refuges.

Maori used many different kinds of defensible position, usually with an outlook over cleared land or water, so they could detect an approaching enemy. Thus the clifftop pa, defended from the sea by the cliffs and from inland by the ditch and bank. Such pa, depending both on a steep natural feature and on some artificial construction, were built in many places including the steep banks of rivers.

The interior construction of the pa might be a succession of ditches and banks, with a confusing entrance, which placed an intruder in a form of maze, attempting to find a way through each succeeding wall. Often the narrow gateways were over-looked by tall fighting-stages from which rocks could be thrown down on attackers.

Inside the pa levelled areas, still detectable today, marked the position of houses and storage places. On hill pa such flattened areas might extend into terraces, each carrying its own defensive wall.

Many of the pits remaining on the terraces of these pa were once kumara stores, dug into the ground perhaps a metre and a half or more in depth but originally roofed. Now they are largely filled with earth, their edges broken down by farm stock, but their regular shapes and placement are still a conspicuous sign of an old Maori position. At the top of the pa was the tihi, an area where the chief lived, and a place where the women who carried the bloodlines of the tribe were sequestered during battle. The tihi was supposedly the last place to fall when the pa came under attack.

Often, however, the battle ended before the pa was properly taken. Many pa could not be defended for long, anyway, as they lacked a natural spring of water to refresh the occupants. Maori fighting often took a ritual form, exacting revenge (utu) or punishment (muru). Battles were of short duration and a defending group, under attack from a superior force, might escape from the pa and vanish into the bush, its numbers largely intact and able to fight again another day.

Maori warfare traditionally involved hand to hand fighting. The wooden fortresses might be too hard to take full frontally. There are many tales of conquering through trickery instead. Defenders were sometimes challenged to come out of their pa and meet in hand-to-hand combat. Such battles might be fought out symbolically by the leading warriors of both sides meeting in a duel.

On other occasions warriors penetrated the pa by arriving in the guise of friends. Then when the hosts slept the invaders rose and killed the occupants making off with their prizes, in the form of women, slaves, valued weapons and food. The spirit of the defeated people was duly assimilated by the conquerors, through taking the leading women, violating the tribal bloodlines, and eating the hearts of defeated chiefs, thereby absorbing their strengths.

Archaeologists have developed a system for classifying pa, according to their position and structure. For the lay person, the discovery of a pa site and a reflective reconstruction of its parameters, can be a fascinating exercise. The position of walls and the number of ditches can give an outline of its layout. Worn pathways up to and through the walls may indicate the position of entrances. The accumulation of house sites and kumara pits fills in some of the living detail of the site. The flattened area at the top can be imagined

TIHI

The top of the pa pictured opposite. This pa is one of a series dug into the ridges of the Papamoa Hills. Adjacent spurs have been flattened for house sites. Palisades of logs topped the surrounding banks and the scarps of terrace edges. On the top, horizontal lines indicate the position of houses and kumara pits. At the far end is the last defended area, the tihi. Traditionally, this is the place where the chief dwelt, and the chietainly women protected. The pa was not conquered until the tihi was taken.

as the central marae and living quarters of the chief and his family. Look to adjacent hills for the pa of other settlements. Some of these pa were used as a defensive position at different times by the same people as they moved about following the seasons or with their shifting horticulture.

The great terraced pa built on the volcanoes of Auckland may not have been occupied all at the same time. Records tell of shifting horticulture and of people moving from volcano to volcano as the fertile soil at the foot of each mountain became exhausted by successive crops. Laying fallow for 15 or so years, the soil would then recover under the regrowth of scrub and the cycle could then repeat.

By far the greater number of fighting pa are situated in the North Island of New Zealand. More than 5500 have been recorded there. The 500 or so pa in the South Island include such landmarks as the Onawe Peninsula in Akaroa Harbour, and the cliff-top pa at Kaikoura much of it now eroded away.

The larger number of pa in the north — and they seem to command every suitable hill, ridge, and cliff in the farthest north — is attributed to the regional culture, based on the ability to grow kumara and store it. In the south such horticulture was generally impossible because of the colder climate. So a wandering people sought food from a succession of places about the countryside and coast without 'settling down' to the same degree.

Only since the introduction of European animals and plants have Maori ceased to rely on hunting and gathering food in the south. The introduction of pigs, goats and chickens, by Captain Cook and others in the eighteenth century, created a new economy, making Maori less dependent on foods they must gather by the season. European plants that would grow in colder climates made horticulture possible in frosty areas. Thus the potato became the kumara of the south. Southern Maori were now more able to settle in one place, just as those in the warmest areas had been able to, through growing tropical vegetables. From the late eighteenth century seeds of several green vegetables were introduced and some even ran wild, available to be gathered by the traveller, or purposely grown in creek beds and gardens. Water cress and wild vegetables like mustards and carrots and Good King Henry are signs of that past still to be found in roadside weed beds.

So the southern pa tend to belong to this later period, when introduced crops provided more staple foods. Yet the move to the coast for fishing and shellfish, and the cycle of travels into the forests and swamps in search of fish and birds and plants, remained regular parts of Maori life in subsistence communities even into the twentieth century.

DITCHES AND BANKS

Ditches and banks are a typical sign of Maori defences. Ditches were dug for protection and to accentuate the height of each successive wall. The steep banks were topped with palisades of logs making them virtually impossible to surmount. Attackers had to breach the walls and struggle up a succession of scarps and banks each with its own palisade. These ditches and banks defend the inland approaches to Turuturumokai Pa near Hawera, South Taranaki.

DEFENDED HILLS

The small volcanic mountains of the north were frequently used as natural defensive sites by Maori. In Auckland, the small volcanoes which dominate the city were heavily defended. Earthworks are obvious on the flanks of the hills, as here on Maungakiekie or One Tree Hill. Like a number of other volcanoes, Maungakiekie had several defended areas about the rim of its crater, each separated by ditches and banks. Attackers would have to fight their way up the mountain then around the rim from fort to fort.

HEADLAND PA

At left: These pa sites are surrounded by the sea and steep cliffs. Both pa have been built on small headlands jutting into Te Kouma Harbour on Coromandel Peninsula. The usual entrance was through the heavily defended landward connexion.

DEFENDED RIDGES

At right: a view of the heavily defended border country between Arawa and Ngaiterangi at Papamoa, Bay of Plenty, taken from the main defended ridge. Earthworks can be traced on the hillock in the foreground. Terraces rise up the spurs of the ridge in the middle ground. Ditches and scarps have been cut across the ridge line to protect a series of hilltop areas overlooking the valleys. Modern horticulture now obscures the ancient fields and a house occupies the top of a defendable hill. The people who lived here were constantly alert to attack. On the higher ridge from which this picture was taken the defences run for some 5 kilometres.

Turuturumokai Pa, near Hawera in South Taranaki, is surrounded on three sides by a deep stream and on the fourth side by substantial banks and ditches. The extensive living terraces are also edged by banks and ditches that once carried palisades. The ditches are clearly defined following 'restoration' by unemployed workers during the 1930s. The ditches of most other pa have been largely filled by erosion and damage by farmstock since being abandoned.

Defensive positions on flat and rolling land were usually simple. A surrounding ditch and bank enclosed a relatively small area, known as a ring ditch pa (right). Both these small defences are near the coast in southern Taranaki.

Clifftop pa on Mount Maunganui (Muao) overlooks Tauranga Harbour. The pa is defended from the hill side by deep ditches and banks still detectable just beyond the fence. The ditches then turn to the clifftop which forms the fourth side of the defences.

At right: Kawau is an island pa in northern Taranaki, protected by cliffs and surrounded by water at high tide. Access was by climbing ropes drawn up behind the defenders. Maori made use of even smaller islets as 'refuge pa' for women and children during battles.

CHANGING TIMES

With the advent of European firearms the defences of the Maori pa were rapidly modified. Ditches now became rifle pits, with the defenders shooting out beneath the palisades. The wooden walls now functioned mainly as a means to hide the positions of defenders, rather than as defensive barriers. The introduction of rockets and artillery in clashes between British and Maori led to further modification of the pa.

RUAPEKAPEKA PA (left)

The first of the New Zealand wars was fought about the Bay of Islands district in 1845-46. At Ruapekapeka (left) the defenders responded to artillery by digging bomb-proof shelters within their pa. In these big holes, protected by roofs of logs, Maori took shelter when not occupying the defensive trenches.

TE PORERE PA (at right)

This fortification near Ruapehu was built for Te Kooti in the closing stages of a campaign to capture him in 1869. It closely resembles the stockades built by Government forces and was basically a system of trenches, parapets and protruding corners, allowing for crossfire. Maori fortification during the North Island wars was carefully recorded by British and Government troops. Consequently, some credit Maori with inventing the techniques of trench warfare later used in the First World War.

Heritage of Aotearoa

CHANGING TIMES 2

Aoraki, at left, is the most sacred of the mountains of the Ngai Tahu people, of the South Island. For long known as Mount Cook, this tallest of New Zealand mountains is now known firstly as Aoraki. The change was decided by the Crown as one way of restoring the traditional links between the tribe and its treasures. Putting the Maori name ahead of a particularly significant English name was one instance of the degree of recognition offered to restore tribal mana following a claim under the Treaty of Waitangi. The treaty settlement also offered Ngai Tahi special advisory rights over the mountain and the right to be consulted about any measures affecting it. Other aspects of the Treaty settlement included restoring Maori names to 47 other natural features, alongside their English ones, to recognise the special relationship between the people and the land.

THE PAST STILL LIVES IN TRADITIONAL THINKING. The ancestors speak to the living. The landscape is imbued with the lives of the people before. Life is faced from the perspective of the backward glance, the memories of the past guiding actions into the future. As more Maori rediscover their heritage more people are demanding a determining influence in how we respect the past.

Claims to the Treaty of Waitangi Tribunal often dwell on the restoration of links between people and their land. In this context the physical signs of the past may help define ancestral connexions with the land and its natural features. Unfortunately, the renaissance comes too late to save many places.

In recent years, rapid change has particularly affected the landscape. Increasingly open spaces have been tamed as farms, built upon, or reclothed in exotic plantations. In the circumstances it is perhaps surprising that so many signs of the pre-European past remain.

It is 200 years since incoming Europeans introduced their technologies. The consequences among Maori were swift and revolutionary.

Guns changed the modes of warfare and altered the political map of the various tribal nations in a few short years. The function of Maori pa rapidly changed to a defensive system of trenches and bomb-proof shelters as it became possible to kill at a distance. Many of the surviving pa show signs of such adaptation.

Agriculture changed too. New temperate plants made gardening possible

in colder places. Introduced vegetables, such as potatoes and sweet corn, changed the substance of staple foods. Traditional foods, such as kumara and taro, were re-introduced with new and more productive strains. Chickens and farm stock supplied new sources of protein. While the patterns of traditional hunting, fishing and gardening survived into the twentieth century, they were largely sustained by new tools and practices. So, as the technological revolution swept the country, the traditions of Aotearoa evolved into a new culture.

The recent process of settling the differences between Maori tribes and the Crown has brought new emphasis upon the dual geography of New Zealand. Yet, while sacred places are acknowledged and ancient names reinstated, the physical signs of the Maori past decay. Despite more effective planning laws, and reorganised protection agencies, there are still not enough resources to protect our common heritage. The challenge of preserving built features remains as difficult in the Maori context as it does in the European landscape. So the signs of the Maori past are at risk along with the buildings and historic places of later settlers.

CHANGING TIMES 3

Cave art reflecting the arrival of a foreign culture. The sailing ship and man on horseback have been added beside more ancient drawings at Takiroa shelter in North Otago. Later visitors have also added their graffiti. Many drawings have been destroyed by casual visitors to the cave sites. Management of several at-risk sites was part of the Treaty settlement proposed to the Ngai Tahu of the South Island.

Further reading and references

HERE IS A SELECTION OF BOOKS which provide helpful information about life in early Aotearoa, and its archaeology. It is not a bibliography, for the references to this period should include many hundreds of academic papers and publications. Some books are categorised under the related chapters in this book. Titles listed under 'Pre-European Life', 'Archaeology', and 'Popular Prehistory' contain more general information.

PRE-EUROPEAN LIFE

Elsdon Best is the author of a series of invaluable monographs published by the Government Printer for the Dominion Museum. The titles provide wide-ranging surveys of information about Maori life and culture gathered in the field in the nineteenth and early twentieth century. Particularly useful background to this book is contained in *The Pa Maori, Forest Lore and the Maori* and *Maori Agriculture*. The series also includes volumes on religion and mythology, traditional knowledge, time, astronomy and navigation; also the material culture including stone implements, storehouses, canoes, fishing and pastimes.

ARCHAEOLOGY

The Prehistory of New Zealand by Janet Davidson (Longman Paul, Auckland 1984). Serious but readable review of researches.

The First Thousand Years, regional perspectives in New Zealand archaeology edited by Nigel Prickett (Dunmore Press, Palmerston North 1982). Summaries of archaeological investigations in most regions of New Zealand.

When all the moa-ovens grew cold by Atholl Anderson (Otago Heritage Books, Dunedin 1983). Readable account of 'nine centuries of changing fortune for the southern Maori'.

POPULAR PREHISTORIES

From the Beginning: The Archaeology of the Maori edited by John Wilson (Penguin Books and the New Zealand Historic Places Trust, Auckland 1987). A symposium by experts, with many artefacts illustrated.

Shadows on the Land: Signs of the Maori Past by Gordon Ell (Bush Press, Auckland 1989) A popular outline of archaeological sites and Maori life before European settlement.

Unearthing New Zealand by Michael Trotter and Beverley McCulloch (GP Books, Wellington 1989). Popular account of archaeological investigations in New Zealand extending into European times and sites.

THE FIRST NEW ZEALANDERS

The Great New Zealand Myth by D. R. Simmons (Reed, Wellington 1976). A scholarly and detailed analysis of Maori tradition which explores the canoe migrations of Polynesians to Aotearoa. Complicated but fundamental to an appreciation of tribal traditions.

LANDMARKS AND PLACENAMES

Tribal Maori histories, of which there are an increasing number, frequently describe the landmarks of their region and relate the stories and people connected with them. There are several books which deal in detail with landmarks and their associated traditions. Notable among them are:

Landmarks of Tainui: Nga Tohu o Tainui by F. L. Phillips, in two privately published volumes (Tohu Publications, Otorohanga). Extensive surveys of the region from Auckland and Coromandel to northern Taranaki, with colour photographs of pa and other sites, and text recording their associated traditions.

LANDMARKS & PLACENAMES (cont'd)

Landmarks of Arawa by Don Stafford (Reed, Auckland 1994). Now two volumes in a similar vein dealing with that Bay of Plenty region.

New Zealand Historical Atlas (Bateman, Auckland 1997) contains maps of prehistoric New Zealand and its resources.

Nga Reo o te Whenua, The Voices of the Land: what place names tells us about our past (no author given) (Learning Media, Wellington 1992). A school classroom resource of teaching and learning ideas, which demonstrates interesting living links between land and people.

Nga Tohu Pumahara, The Survey Pegs of the Past: Understanding Maori Place Names (New Zealand Geographic Board, Wellington 1990). Compiled by Te Aue Davies, Tipene O'Regan and John Wilson. A fascinating insight into the naming of places in Aotearoa.

LIVING OFF THE LAND, WILD CROPS etc

Forest Lore of the Maori by Elsdon Best (Government Printer, Wellington 1977). (Dominion Museum Bulletin No. 14) Detailed account 'with methods of snaring, trapping, and preserving birds and rats, uses of berries, roots, fern-root, and forest products with mythological notes on origins, karakia used etc.'

Greenstone Trails: The Maori Search for Pounamu by Barry Brailsford (Stoneprint Press, Hamilton, 1997). Interesting account of Maori trails through the Southern Alps.

The Natural World of the Maori by Margaret Orbell, photographs Geoff Moon (Bateman, Auckland 1996). A popular pictorial survey of Maori and their dependence on the natural world.

MAORI ROCK ART

Prehistoric Rock Art of New Zealand by Michael Trotter and Beverley McCulloch (Longman Paul, Auckland 1981). (New Zealand Archaeological Association Monograph No. 12). Scholarly but readable introduction to the subject.

MORIORI

Moriori: a people rediscovered by Michael King (Viking, Auckland 1989). A lively history of the Moriori people of the Chatham islands, New Zealand's 'other' Eastern Polynesian culture.

MAORI GARDENING, KUMARA etc

Maori Agriculture by Elsdon Best (Government Printer, Wellington 1976). (Dominion Museum Bulletin No. 9) Detailed account of 'the cultivated food plants of the natives of New Zealand, with some account of native methods of agriculture, its ritual and origin myths'.

1000 Years of Gardening in New Zealand by Helen Leach, illustrated Nancy Tichborne (Reed, Wellington 1984). About half of this well-illustrated book, written by an archaeologist, is concerned with Maori gardening practices.

MAORI PA

Nga Tohuwhenua Mai Te Rangi: a New Zealand archaeology in aerial photographs by Kevin L. Jones (Victoria University Press, Wellington 1994). Extensive aerial coverage of Maori sites, organised by region, plus some European settlement.

The Pa Maori by Elsdon Best (Government Printer, Wellington 1975). (Dominion Museum Bulletin No. 6) Detailed account of 'fortified villages of the Maori in pre-European and modern times; illustrating methods of defence by means of ramparts, fosses, scarps and stockades'.

Prehistoric Maori Fortifications in the North Island of New Zealand by Aileen Fox (Longman Paul, Auckland 1976.1978). (New Zealand Archaeological Association Monograph No. 6). An expert's survey of pa sites and types, including some comparisons with Celtic forts in Britain.

The Tattooed Land: the Southern Frontiers of the Pa Maori by Barry Brailsford (Reed, Wellington 1981). Detailed, well-illustrated survey of Maori pa in the South Island.

Index

Generally relates to specific sites; or localities where more appropriate. Placenames are listed in Maori and English if both are commonly used in the text. (e.g. Maungawhau, Mt Eden). **Illustrations indicated in bold type.**

Names of the Plants

THE COMMON NAMES OF PLANTS used in the text are given here with their Maori, English and Latin equivalents, for more detailed reference. Regarding the Maori names: these may vary in tribal dialects but in each case, here, the words used are those generally accepted as the common names for the plants.

Aute, paper mulberry, *Broussonetia papyrifera*
Bracken root, aruhe, *Pteridium esculentum*
Bulrush, raupo, *Typha orientalis*
Cabbage tree, ti, ti kouka etc, *Cordyline* spp.
Flax, harakeke, *Phormium tenax.*
Gourd, hue, *Lagenaria siceraria*
formerly *Lagenaria vulgaris*
Harakeke, flax, *Phormium tenax*
Hue, gourd, *Lagenaria siceraria*
Kahikatea, white pine, *Dacrycarpus dacrydiodes,* formerly *Podocarpus dacrydiodes*
Kaikomako, *Pennantia corymbosa*
Karaka, *Corynocarpus laevigatus*
Kawakawa, northern pepper plant, *Macropiper excelsum*
Kopi (Chathams), karaka, *Corynocarpus laevigatus*
Kumara, sweet potato, *Ipomoea batatas*
Mountain flax, wharariki, *Phormium cookianum*
Nikau, *Rhopalostylis sapida*
Paper mulberry, aute, *Broussonetia papyrifera*
Pingao, golden sand sedge, *Desmoschoenus spiralis*
Raupo, bulrush, *Typha orientalis*
Rimu, red pine, *Dacrydium cupressinum*
Seaweeds, kohukohu, rehia, rimurimu. Algae
Sweet potato, kumara, *Ipomoea batatas*
Taro, *Colacasia esculenta*
Ti, Cabbage tree, *Cordyline* spp.
Toetoe *Cortaderia* spp. etc.
Totara, *Podocarpus totara*
Whau, *Entelea aborescens*
Yam, *Dioscorea alata*

GORDON ELL has been making films and writing books about the natural and historic heritage of New Zealand for 25 years. Brought up in the South Island back country, he presently lives in Takapuna but travels widely within New Zealand, working in the outdoors. His interest in pre-European New Zealand is reflected in a previous book about signs of the Maori past called *Shadows on the Land* and television features including *The People Before* which led to his being made an Associate of the Royal Photographic Society. GORDON ELL has been a member of several parks and reserves boards, the New Zealand Conservation Authority, national president of the Royal Forest and Bird Protection Society and a trustee of Auckland War Memorial Museum.

THE BUSH PRESS HISTORIC PLACES OF NEW ZEALAND SERIES

Heritage of Aotearoa is the first in a proposed series of books about the historic landscapes and buildings of New Zealand. Author-photographer GORDON ELL is presently working on a volume about 'Discovery and Adventure', featuring the landing places of early explorers and the sites of early European settlement, from sealers and timbermen in the 1790s, to whaling and mission stations prior to the Treaty of Waitangi in 1840.

Other books by GORDON ELL include:

King Kauri: Tales and Traditions of the Kauri Country
Gold Rush: Tales and Traditions of the New Zealand Goldfields
New Zealand Traditions and Folklore
New Zealand Ghost Towns and Glimpses of the Past
Gold Rush Country of New Zealand
Shadows on the Land: Signs of the Maori Past
Wild Islands of the Hauraki Gulf
Encouraging Birds in the New Zealand Garden
Enjoying Nature in the New Zealand Garden
Seashore Birds of New Zealand (with G.J.H. Moon)
Nature Hobbies for New Zealanders
Introduced Wildflowers, New Zealand Weeds
The *Discover New Zealand* Series
and contributions to:
The Natural History of Auckland
Reader's Digest Book of Wild New Zealand
Children's books include:
The *Children's Guides to Nature* Series
The *Waiatarua Wild Wonders* Series
Wainamu: the Town by the Sea
Abel Tasman: In Search of the Great South Land
New Zealand's Story in Stamps